How It's Built
SKYSCRAPER

by Vicky Franchino

Illustrations by Richard Watson

Children's Press®
An imprint of Scholastic Inc.

Thanks to Donald Friedman, PE, Fellow of the American Society of Civil Engineers, for his role as content consultant for this book.

Thanks to Donna Lowich, Senior Information Specialist at the Christopher & Dana Reeve Foundation, for her insights into the daily lives of people who use wheelchairs.

Library of Congress Cataloging-in-Publication Data
Names: Franchino, Vicky, author. | Watson, Richard, 1980– illustrator.
Title: How it's built. Skyscraper/by Vicky Franchino; illustrated by Richard Watson.
Other titles: Skyscraper
Description: First edition. | New York, NY: Children's Press, an imprint of Scholastic Inc., 2022. | Includes index. | Audience: Ages 5–7 | Audience: Grades K–1 | Summary: "Narrative nonfiction with fictional characters who visit various work sites to find out how skyscrapers are built. Full-color illustrations and photographs throughout"—Provided by publisher.
Identifiers: LCCN 2021029555 (print) | LCCN 2021029556 (ebook) | ISBN 9781338800067 (library binding) | ISBN 9781338800098 (paperback) | ISBN 9781338800104 (ebk)
Subjects: LCSH: Skyscrapers—Design and construction—Juvenile literature. | BISAC: JUVENILE NONFICTION/Technology/How Things Work–Are Made
Classification: LCC TH1615 .F73 2022 (print) | LCC TH1615 (ebook) | DDC 720/.483—dc23
LC record available at https://lccn.loc.gov/2021029555
LC ebook record available at https://lccn.loc.gov/2021029556

Copyright © 2022 by Scholastic Inc.

All rights reserved. Published by Children's Press, an imprint of Scholastic Inc., *Publishers since 1920*.
SCHOLASTIC, CHILDREN'S PRESS, HOW IT'S BUILT™, and associated logos are trademarks and/or registered trademarks of Scholastic Inc.

The publisher does not have any control over and does not assume any responsibility for author or third-party websites or their content.

No part of this publication may be reproduced, stored in a retrieval system, or transmitted in any form or by any means, electronic, mechanical, photocopying, recording, or otherwise, without written permission of the publisher.
For information regarding permission, write to Scholastic Inc.,
Attention: Permissions Department, 557 Broadway,
New York, NY 10012.

10 9 8 7 6 5 4 3 2 1   22 23 24 25 26

Printed in the U.S.A.   113
First edition, 2022

Series produced by Spooky Cheetah Press
Book design by Maria Bergós, Book & Look
Page design by Kathleen Petelinsek, The Design Lab

Photos ©: cover: Asia Photopress/Alamy Images; 5 top: Courtesy of RWDI; 5 bottom right: Jon Arnold Images Ltd/Alamy Images; 6: Topdeq/Dreamstime; 10–11 blueprint: Courtesy of COOP HIMMELB(L)AU; 12–13: Dontworry/Wikimedia; 13 inset: Courtesy of RWDI; 16 left: Steve P./Alamy Images; 18–19: Jjfarq/Dreamstime; 21 inset: tomczykbartek/Getty Images; 22–23: blickwinkel/Alamy Images; 24–25: Thomas Lohnes/Getty Images; 26–27: Jon Arnold Images Ltd/Alamy Images; 29 bottom left: Gilles Malo/Dreamstime; 31 top right: Juergen Hasenkopf/Alamy Images.

All other photos © Shutterstock.

TABLE OF CONTENTS

Meet the Junior Engineers Club...........4

Let's Build a Skyscraper!....................6

Machinery and Tools for
Building a Skyscraper......................28

Skyscrapers Built in Amazing Ways........30

Index...32

About the Author..........................32

MEET THE JUNIOR ENGINEERS CLUB

Sofia · Lucas · Kai · Nisha · Jacob · Zoe

These six friends love learning about how things are built! This is their workshop.

Nisha and Jacob found out how a skyscraper is built. Now they are sharing what they learned!

It can take many years to plan and build a skyscraper.

PROJECTS
HOUSE
CAR
BRIDGE
SKYSCRAPER
ROCKET
SAILBOAT

Jacob and I visited the construction company that worked on our city's new skyscraper. First, we talked to Mateo. He is the architect who designed the building.

Mateo told us a different building used to be on the spot where the new building is now. A work crew tore it down.

A skyscraper has a small footprint. That means it does not take up much space on the ground. But because the building is so tall, many people can live or work in it.

Mateo told us that architects used to draw buildings with pens and pencils. Now they use computers. A blueprint is a drawing of the skyscraper.

Could you make the building look any way you wanted?

10

Lily told us a skyscraper must be very strong. It has to support the weight of the building as well as the weight of everything inside it. She told us about some of the materials that are used to build a skyscraper.

Concrete is made of cement, water, and rocks. It can be formed into many shapes. Concrete starts as a liquid. When concrete dries, it is hard and strong. The center of the skyscraper is made of concrete.

Steel is light and strong and can also be made into many shapes. Steel makes a good building frame. The frame is like the skeleton of the skyscraper.

Steel rods are added to concrete to make it even stronger. This is called **reinforced concrete**. It is used in the foundation of a skyscraper. The foundation is at the bottom and supports the rest of the building.

Aluminum is a metal that is lighter than steel. It won't rust if it gets wet. That is why aluminum is a good choice for the outside of a building.

What material is the most common for building?

Concrete! It is used for buildings of all different types and sizes.

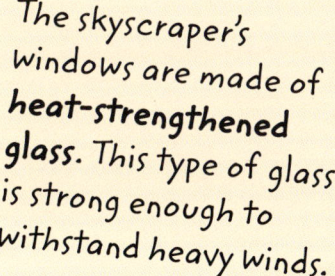

The skyscraper's windows are made of **heat-strengthened glass**. This type of glass is strong enough to withstand heavy winds.

After the skyscraper was designed, building began. Jayden was the general contractor. It was his job to manage all the different people who built the skyscraper. The first thing they did was lay the foundation.

1 Workers dug a big hole in the ground until they hit rock. Having a layer of rock under the foundation keeps the skyscraper from sinking into the ground. Most skyscraper foundations are deep.

2 After the hole was dug, workers poured the concrete foundation. It took many hours to fill the hole with concrete.

Next came the framework, which holds up the skyscraper. Tall columns were attached to the foundation. They support the building's weight. Then beams were attached to the columns. They hold up the floors and roof. Finally, braces were added to make the framework strong.

The outside of the building is called the curtain wall. It covers and protects everything inside!

Skyscrapers are sometimes built where there might be an earthquake. A damper is a heavy weight inside the building. It sways back and forth to keep the building from moving too much when the earth is shaking.

19

Once the framework was in place, we watched ironworkers attach sheets of reinforcing steel mesh to the beams.

Then concrete was pumped through long hoses up to the steel mesh. Workers smoothed it out to make floors and ceilings.

A special pump pushes the concrete up to the high floors of a skyscraper.

Jayden explained that a lot is hidden inside the walls of a skyscraper. Pipes move water. Tubes called ducts deliver warm and cold air throughout the skyscraper. Wires carry the electricity that makes lights and computers work.

Water

Sprinkler sytem

Electricity

Drain

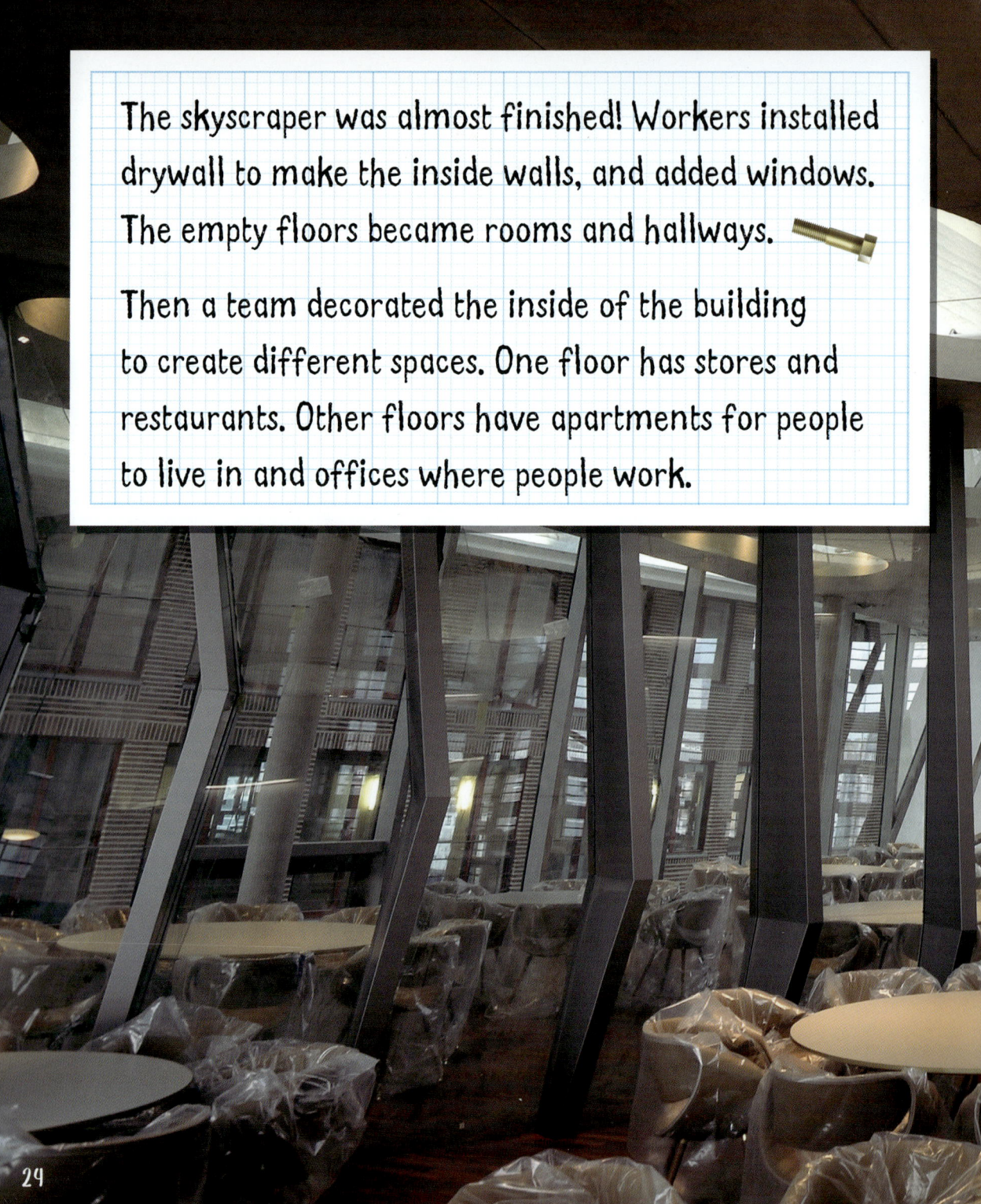

The skyscraper was almost finished! Workers installed drywall to make the inside walls, and added windows. The empty floors became rooms and hallways.

Then a team decorated the inside of the building to create different spaces. One floor has stores and restaurants. Other floors have apartments for people to live in and offices where people work.

Even when the skyscraper is finished, the work never stops. Engineers check the building and fix anything that gets broken. There are many, many windows to wash, too. Sometimes the window washers hang from ropes to work (pictured). Sometimes they use platforms that hang from ropes.

MACHINERY AND TOOLS FOR BUILDING A SKYSCRAPER

Jackhammer
This tool is used to break up concrete and other hard materials.

Excavator
Workers use this heavy machine to dig the foundation.

Concrete Mixer
This special truck is used to mix, carry, and pour the wet concrete.

Safety Equipment
A hard hat protects the workers from falling debris. A safety harness keeps them from falling off the building!

Crane
This machine raises and lowers materials at the building site.

Hoist
A hoist carries people and equipment between the floors of the skyscraper.

Scaffolding
Workers stand on this platform while building or repairing the skyscraper.

29

SKYSCRAPERS BUILT IN AMAZING WAYS

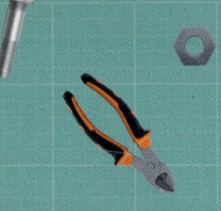

At 1,483 ft. (452 m), the **Petronas Towers** in Kuala Lumpur, Malaysia, are the tallest twin skyscrapers. Each tower has a concrete frame that helps keep the building from moving too much in the wind.

The **Empire State Building** in New York City is 1,250 ft. (381 m) tall. Assembly lines made it possible to build this skyscraper very quickly. Each construction worker had one special job to do over and over.

The **Shard** is the tallest building in London, England. It is 1,016 ft. (310 m) tall. A shard is a sharp piece of glass, and that is what this building looks like! The outside of the Shard is covered in 11,000 pieces of glass.

The taller of the two **Le Nouvel** residential towers in Kuala Lumpur, Malaysia, is 656 ft. (200 m) tall. But that's not what makes this skyscraper so amazing. Both towers are covered with vertical forests that are made up of 243 species of plants.

The **Bitexco Financial Tower** is in Ho Chi Minh City in Vietnam. It is 861 ft. (263 m) tall. A landing pad for helicopters, called a helipad, sticks out from the 55th floor of the building. The helipad was built on the ground and pulled into place!

31

INDEX

aluminum 15
Bitexco Financial Tower 31
blueprint 10, 11
Burj Khalifa 7
Capital Gate 6
concrete 14, 15, 16, 20, 21, 28, 30
concrete mixer 28
crane 29
curtain wall 18
damper 19
drywall 24
ducts 22

electricity 17, 22
Empire State Building 30
excavator 28
footprint 9
foundation 15, 16, 17, 18, 28
framework 18, 20
hoist 29
ironworkers 20
jackhammer 28
Le Nouvel towers 31
light bulbs 25
megatall skyscrapers 7

One World Trade Center 7
Petronas Towers 30
pipes 22
safety equipment 29
scaffolding 29
Shard, the 31
steel 14, 15, 20
supertall skyscrapers 7
utilities 17, 22, 23
wind 13, 15, 30
wind tunnel 13
windows 15, 24, 27

ABOUT THE AUTHOR

Vicky Franchino has written many books for children. She has been to some very tall buildings, but Vicky is a little afraid of heights. She would not want to wash windows on a skyscraper!